Coming Up For Air

*Thoughts to Lift the Spirit
and Refresh the Soul*

Mary Murray Shelton

Copyright © 2014 Mary Murray Shelton

All rights reserved.

ISBN: 10 1499383088
ISBN-13: 978-1499383089

DEDICATION

For those who thirst for the divine connection
through words and images, music, sacred sites,
lovers, art, flowers and beauty,
these writers have gone before us to encourage us
and to help light the path.

This collection is dedicated to you and to them.

CONTENTS

	Acknowledgments	i
	Introduction	iii
1	Transformation	1
2	Beckoning	13
3	Creativity and Play	23
4	Persistence	40
5	Gratitude and Grace	51
6	Love	62
7	Letting Go	73
8	Oneness	94
9	Spiritual Maturity	105
10	Truth	115
	About the Author	125
	Index of Those Quoted	126

ACKNOWLEDGMENTS

Thank you to Joel Fotinos, who directed me to *Create Space*,
to Karyl Huntley who encouraged me to do this collection,
and to Amanda Kreglow,
my constant cheerleader and life companion.

INTRODUCTION

As a professional speaker who is always creating new presentations, I liberally sprinkle my talks with quotes that clarify or introduce my points, stimulate thinking, or touch the hearts of those listening.

The quotes that I've chosen to share with you in this collection are some of those that I like the best and use the most. I hope you will find some of your favorites among them as well.

To begin, I suggest turning to the topic or person that calls to you. An alphabetical list of those who are quoted, with the page numbers their quotes appear on, is at the back of the book.

Or you might find just what you need by opening the book anywhere and beginning there.

Who knows what may be waiting for you in these pages?

1 TRANSFORMATION

Something magic happens to human beings in the change process.

At times the process is awesome and mysterious, like the transformation of a caterpillar into a butterfly.

We seem to be coded to reach for what affects and changes us, forcing us to stretch and become something more than we have known ourselves to be.

Fire transforms all things it touches
into its own nature.

The wood does not change the fire into itself,
but the fire changes the wood into itself.

In the same way, we are transformed into God
so that we may know him as he is.

Acting and becoming are one.
God and I are one in this work,
he acts and I become.

Meister Eckhart

True love is unconquerable and irresistible.
It goes on gathering force
until it transforms everyone it touches.

Meher Baba

For a long time it had seemed to me
that my life was about to begin—real life.
But there was always something in the way,
something to be got through first,
some unfinished business,
time still to be served,
a debt to be paid,
then life would begin.

At last it dawned on me that these
obstacles were my life.

Alfred D'Souza

When I let go of what I am,
I become what I might be.

Lao Tzu

What AM I?
I PRay that I can become what
I might be — But first Must I
Know what I AM? Is knowing what You
Are, ALL Faith in GoD? Is it accepting
That You Were Always A Child of GoD,
ALL good? Or do You listen To Some
Churches Who Says You are born in
Sin and bad?

Only from your heart can you touch the sky.

Jelaluddin Rumi

In your light I learn how to love,
in your beauty, how to make poems.
You dance inside my chest
where no one sees you,
but sometimes I do,
and that sight becomes this art.

There is a candle in your heart,
ready to be kindled.
There is a void in your soul,
ready to be filled.
You feel it, don't you?

Jelaluddin Rumi

Yes — And I know that silent voice within me is God.

...when Mt. Everest was scaled
the phrase commonly used in the West
to describe the feat was
"the conquest of Everest."

An Oriental, whose writings
have been deeply influenced by Taoism, remarked,
"We would put the matter differently.
We would speak of the befriending of Everest."

Huston Smith

Do not be conformed to this age,
but be transformed by the renewing of your mind,
that you may prove what the will of God is,
that which is good and acceptable and perfect.

St. Paul, Letter to the Romans 12:2

There is for us a point at which not growing
means diminishing–
a point at which we can only choose
between despair or change.

Ellen Goodman

[Handwritten note: Despair or Change? Who wants to feel in DARKNESS, So sad Layer and Layers]

It takes courage to grow up
and become who you really are.

e.e. cummings

Never before has there been so much
scientifically based knowledge
about the transformative capacities
of human nature.

This knowledge,
combined with the lore and inspiration
of the sacred traditions,
gives the human race
an unprecedented opportunity
to make a great evolutionary advance.

It is possible now, we believe,
for humanity to pursue its destiny
with more clarity than ever before.

George Leonard & Michael Murphy

2 BECKONING

Just as we seem coded to stretch and grow, there is something that encourages us to do so.

At times this Mystery seems to know us and to draw us forward toward It. At other times It seems to come to get us in synchronicities and coincidences.

What is this Mystery to which we are constantly invited to come closer?

We are more than we seem to be, and we are valued and treasured more than we can imagine.

It is amazing that every atom of our bodies
—*every atom of our bodies*—
was forged in the fire of a star!

I think one of the worst crimes on earth
is that we're not telling every child this. *Every child.*

So instead of having them
identify themselves in some small, little way,
they begin to see themselves as a cosmic event,
assembled out of stars.

Brian Swimme

Come, come, whoever you are.

Wanderer, worshiper, lover of leaving,
it doesn't matter.
Ours is not a caravan of despair.

Come,
even if you have broken your vows
a thousand times.

Come yet again,
come,
come.

Jelaluddin Rumi

It has taken fifteen billion years
to get you here.
That is scientific fact.

We are not just the products of our parents.

Sixty percent of our body is hydrogen atoms.
The hydrogen atoms in us go back
to the fireball fourteen billion years ago.

We have been around a long time,
and it has been a great birthing process
to bring us forward.

Matthew Fox

Every blade of grass has its own angel
bending over it
whispering,
Grow, grow.

The Talmud

We don't have to be *chosen*
or even to be physically in the presence
of some holy being
to get the benefit
of their transformational consciousness,
teaching and coaching.

We can engage in learning from them
even if they are no longer in the body,
or if they are fictional characters.

Mary Murray Shelton

Listen–perhaps you catch a hint
of an ancient state not quite forgotten;
dim, perhaps
and yet not altogether unfamiliar,
like a song whose name is long forgotten,
and the circumstance in which you heard
completely unremembered.

Not the whole song has stayed with you,
but just a little wisp of melody,
attached not to a person or a place
or anything particular.

But you remember,
from just this little part,
how lovely was the song,
how wonderful the setting
where you heard it,
and how you loved those
who were there and listened with you.

A Course in Miracles

No matter what our emotional storm,
or what our objective situation may be
there is always something hidden
in the inner being
that has never been violated.

We may stumble,
but always is that Eternal Voice,
forever whispering within our ear,
that thing which causes the eternal quest,
that thing which forever sings and sings.

Ernest Holmes

I know you're tired, but come;
this is the way.

Jelaluddin Rumi

We are stardust; we are golden.

Joni Mitchell

3 CREATIVITY AND PLAY

Play comes naturally. Some of us may have forgotten this.

Too many people are under the mistaken impression that they are not *creative* or *artistic*, or that creativity and play are too difficult for the less gifted.

We think we mustn't sing, or play a sport, or write a poem unless we can win an award for doing so. How absurd!

I do not believe any human being ever existed who was not the creative artist of his or her own life. We define creative expression too narrowly.

Delight is the key to creativity and play. What delights you?

I used to think that delight arose
unbidden and unexpectedly
out of some kind of very pleasant surprise.
I realize now that delight is a choice.

It arises when I am present
and welcoming of this moment,
just as it is.

This is a challenge,
but it is possible,
because we are coded to experience delight.

Our job, then,
as divine distributors of God's magnificence,
is to create magic,
but it is also to be recipients of magic,
practitioners of the art of delighting
and being delighted.

Mary Murray Shelton

Living is a form of not being sure,
not knowing what next or how.
The moment you know how you begin to die a little.

The artist never entirely knows, we guess.
We may be wrong, but we take leap after leap in the dark.

Agnes de Mille

The creation of something new
is not accomplished by the intellect
but by the play instinct
acting from inner necessity.

The creative mind plays with the objects it loves.

Carl Jung

How one conceives of what one wants
is deceptively simple and profoundly sophisticated…
every professional creator
either consciously or intuitively
thoroughly understands the principle
of how a creator conceives of a vision.

The creator simply makes up the vision.

While creative people know
that they make up what they create,
there is a strange prejudice in society
against this notion.

Robert Fritz

Creative people are committed to risk.

The creative person
always walks two steps into the darkness.

Everybody can see what's in the light.
They can imitate it, they can underscore it,
they can modify it, they can reshape it.

But the real heroes delve in the darkness
of the unknown.

Benny Golson

Inside you there's an artist you don't know about…

Jelaluddin Rumi

You will find truth more quickly
through delight than gravity.

Let out a little more string on your kite.

Alan Cohen

There is a vitality, a life force, an energy, a quickening,
that is translated through *you* into action…

It is not your business
to determine how good it is,
nor how valuable,
nor how it compares to other expressions.

It is your business to keep the channel open.
You do not even have to believe in yourself or your work.

You have to keep open and aware directly
to the urges that activate you.
Keep the channel open.

Martha Graham

Let the beauty we love be what we do.

There are hundreds of ways
to kneel and kiss the ground.

Jelaluddin Rumi

If we were a medical school,
and you were here as a med student
practicing appendectomies,
you'd take your work very seriously
because you would imagine that some night at 2:00 AM
someone is going to waltz into your emergency room
and you're going to have to save their life.

Well, my friends,
someday at 8:00 PM
someone is going to walk into your concert hall
and bring you a mind that is confused,
a heart that is overwhelmed,
a soul that is weary.

Whether they go out whole again
will depend partly on how well you do your craft.

Karl Paulnack

Looking at God's creation,
it is pretty clear
that the creator itself
did not know when to stop.

There is not one pink flower,
or even fifty pink flowers,
but hundreds.

Snowflakes, of course,
are the ultimate exercise
in sheer creative glee.
No two alike.

This creator looks suspiciously like someone
who just might send us support
for our creative ventures.

Julia Cameron

Creativity is God's nature;
therefore the Universe is constantly
in the process of creating,
becoming,
and being created.

The Universe *must* continuously create newness
in order for God to be constantly expressing Its nature.

Newness is always available.
As we create and experience newness,
we are, in a sense, creating God
—creating more of the expressed "body" of God—
and giving God a bigger portal
through which to be expressed.

Mary Murray Shelton

All true artists, whether they know it or not,
create from a place of no-mind, from inner stillness.

Eckhart Tolle

There is a laughter of God—let's laugh it…
There is a song of the universe—let's sing it.
There is a deep, abiding peace;
let's experience it.

Ernest Holmes

When you do things from your soul
you feel a river moving in you
a joy.

Jelaluddin Rumi

The reason we like precious jewels so much is
they remind us of planes of consciousness we've lived on,
where those are the pebbles.

Aldous Huxley

4 PERSISTENCE

Persistence wears parents out, so children are often discouraged from being persistent. They might be punished, scolded or embarrassed until the tendency is trained out of them.

We need to reclaim persistence to live fully. Persistence is the antidote to discouragement and cynicism because it arises out of commitment and intention that are connected to a greater vision of life.

Persistence renews us so that we can begin again when a particular effort has failed.

It means not giving up too soon. It means assuming that there is a way, and that the way can be found.

Expectancy speeds progress.
Therefore live in a continual state of expectancy.
No matter how much good you are experiencing today,
expect greater good tomorrow…

It makes life a game that is a joy to play.
It enables you to enter into the spirit
of things and of people.

Ernest Holmes

Founder of Science of Mind

Failure is the path of least persistence.

George M. Van Valkenburg, Jr.

The difference between
a pipe dream
and a great idea
is persistence.

Unknown

Nearly every man who develops an idea
works at it
up to the point where it looks impossible,
and then gets discouraged.

That's not the place to become discouraged.

Thomas A. Edison

*Seek and you shall find,
knock and the door will be opened,
ask and it shall be given...*

It sounds like the point of the story
is that it's okay to ask,
and that asking will be rewarded.

But this Bible verse follows a longer story
in which the point is not just asking,
but asking persistently until one obtains results.

Not only is it okay to ask, the story says,
but also it goes on to exhort the listeners
to persist in asking, knocking and seeking
until they receive
that for which they are searching.

Mary Murray Shelton

A Science of Mind
Minister & Writer

I have lived on the lip of insanity,
wanting to know reasons,
knocking on a door.

It opens.

I've been knocking from the inside.

Jelaluddin Rumi

The person who is a master in the art of living
makes little distinction
between their work and their play,
their labor and their leisure,
their mind and their body,
their education and their recreation,
their love and their religion.

They hardly know which is which.

They simply pursue their vision of excellence and grace
in whatever they do,
leaving others to decide whether
they are working or playing.

To them, they are always doing both.

Zen Buddhism

If you're going through hell, keep going.

Winston Churchill

How much energy does it take for a chick
to break out of an egg?

Half its body weight, at least.

Harriet Rubin

There will come a time
when you believe everything is finished.

That will be the beginning.

Louis L'Amour

5 GRATITUDE AND GRACE

When grace enters our life, it can take our breath away. It appears whole and complete without any clear link to what we have done to attract it. It appears in a timely way and is always very specific to the person and the need.

Some would call this luck, but when we *experience it* that is harder to do. Grace doesn't feel random or meaningless. It feels deliberate: Something is responding directly to us.

The only appropriate response is appreciation, savoring, and entering into the fullness of the experience with gratitude.

Now is the time for the world to know
that every thought and action is sacred.

This is the time for you to deeply compute
the impossibility that there is anything but Grace.

Now is the season to know
that everything you do is sacred.

Hafiz

The Light of God surrounds you.
The Love of God enfolds you.
The Power of God protects you.
The Presence of God is with you.
Wherever you go, God is.

Unity Prayer for Protection

What you seek is seeking you.

Jelaluddin Rumi

God created all things in such a way
that they are not outside himself,
as ignorant people falsely imagine.

Rather, all creatures flow outward,
but nonetheless remain within God.

God created all things this way:
not that they might stand outside of God,
nor beyond God,
but that they might come into God
and receive God
and dwell in God.

For this reason everything that is
is bathed in God,
is enveloped by God,
who is round-about us all,
enveloping us.

Meister Eckhart

Like any other gift,
the gift of grace can be ours
only if we reach out and take it.

Maybe being able to reach out and take it
is a gift too.

Anne Lamott

The search for reason ends
at the shore of the known;
on the immense expanse beyond it
only the sense of the ineffable can glide.

It alone knows the route
to that which is remote from experience
and understanding.

Neither is amphibious;
reason cannot go beyond the shore,
and the sense of the ineffable
is out of place where we measure;
where we weigh…

Abraham Joshua Heschel

What good is it to me
if this eternal birth of the divine Son
takes place unceasingly
but does not take place within myself?

And what good is it to me if Mary is full of grace
and if I am not also full of grace?

What good is it to me
for the Creator to give birth to his/her Son
if I do not also give birth to him
in my time and my culture?

This, then, is the fullness of time:
When the Son of God is begotten in us.

Meister Eckhart

Accept, then act.
Whatever the present moment contains,
accept it as if you had chosen it.
Always work with it, not against it…
This will miraculously transform your whole life.

Eckhart Tolle

I have no son but I remember one
one boy's soft face
a gentle neck I traced with my fingers
and the way his hair felt in my hands
character like a wildflower pushing up
even through youth a kindness sprang
and grace uncommon in green years
still no one avoids the tug and toss of growing
and this heart learns lessons as all hearts do
responding to compassion's call
braving commitment
standing tall on sand, mud, rock, earth
through shifting seasons
coming
going
while through it all
a boy becomes what he is meant to be
and casts the shadow of his own silhouette
upon the lives he loves as shelter
haven
harbor
trading hopes for courage
reaching to take hold and give with both hands
this once-upon-a-time boy
now so much a man
in photographs I've watched his wildflower soul open
across years and miles
face and eyes familiar through change
I do not need to touch his hair
to recognize the person there
though not my son
I know this one

Tinker Donnelly

We do not "come into" this world;
we come out of it, as leaves from a tree.
As the ocean "waves," the universe "peoples."
Every individual is an expression
of the whole realm of nature,
a unique action of the total universe.

Alan Watts

6 LOVE

Love is so pervasively around and in everything that it seems too common or too trite to describe. At the same time, it is the central reason we are here.

We spend lifetimes seeking love, being mesmerized by it or pushing it away. But like the fish looking for water, we can't remove ourselves from it.

We can forget about love's persistent presence, though. The words in this section may remind us.

Your task is not to seek for love,
but merely to seek and find all the barriers
within yourself
that you have built against it.

Jelaluddin Rumi

...it is hard to be loving all the time.
But it's harder not to be loving.

Stephen Levine

The minute I heard my first love story,
I started looking for you,
not knowing how blind that was.

Lovers don't finally meet somewhere.

They're in each other all along.

Jelaluddin Rumi

There are several kinds of galaxies.
The main two are elliptical and spiral…
Spiral galaxies create new stars;
elliptical galaxies don't…

Say you're an elliptical galaxy–
one by one your stars are going to die out…

There's an elliptical galaxy
called the Large Magellanic Cloud.
It was drawn in by the Milky Way [a spiral galaxy],
and as it got involved with the Milky Way dynamics,
it lit up with star birth!
Total surprise!

Isn't that fantastic? Isn't that just great?
You want an image of spirituality–there it is!

Through our encounters we have the possibility
of awakening the deep creative energy
that has either been broken down,
or has fallen asleep,
or hasn't yet seen what it is.

Brain Swimme

There is a polish
for everything that becomes rusty,
and the polish for the heart
is remembrance of God.

Hadith: Sayings of the Prophet

Love is the central flame of the universe.

Ernest Holmes

Let yourself be drawn
by the stronger pull of that which you truly love.

Jelaluddin Rumi

Letting people in is largely a matter
of not spending energy to keep them out.

Hugh Prather

Love is the opening door.

Bernie Taupin

Love is the grandest
healing and drawing power on earth…

From selfish reasons alone,
if from no loftier reason,
we cannot afford to find fault, to hate,
or even to hold in mind
anything against any living soul!

Ernest Holmes

7 LETTING GO

Letting go is one of the primary tasks of our lives.

We live on a planet where everything transforms over time until it returns to atoms and molecules that re-enter the cycle of existence, recombining to become something or someone new. All form is in a continuous state of birth, life, death and rebirth.

Without attachments letting go would be easy. We would notice absences, but feel no anguish over them. But we do get attached.

We will eventually have to release every one of the people, places and things to which we feel attached. Even our own bodies.

Letting go is an ongoing practice. Forgiveness is one of its sacred keys.

By letting it go it all gets done.
The world is won by those who let it go.
But when you try and try
the world is beyond the winning.

Lao Tzu

All spiritual growth, one hundred percent of it,
is about releasing or eliminating
rather than attaining something,
because we're already it spiritually.

Michael Beckwith

Last night as I was sleeping,
I dreamt —*marvelous error!*
—that I had a beehive here inside my heart,
and the golden bees
were making white combs of sweet honey
from my old failures.

Antonio Machado

Nature will not let us stay in any one place too long.
She will let us stay just long enough
to gather the experience necessary
to the unfolding and advancement of the soul.

Ernest Holmes

Courage is the power to let go of the familiar.

Raymond Lindquist

We must be willing to let go of the life we have planned, so as to accept the life that is waiting for us.

Joseph Campbell

The harder you fight to hold on to specific assumptions, the more likely there's gold in letting go of them.

John Seely Brown

Forgiveness does not change the past,
but it does enlarge the future.

Paul Boese

Having a personal opinion is great.
Believing that one's personal opinion
is absolute truth
leads to most of the world's troubles.

Jonathan Lockwood Huie

You wander from room to room
hunting for the diamond necklace
that is already around your neck!

Jelaluddin Rumi

Joy increases
and suffering decreases
as one masters the distinction
between events and one's feelings
about those events.

Jonathan Lockwood Huie

I don't let go of concepts;
I meet them with understanding.
Then they let go of me.

Byron Katie

Suffering is not holding you.
You are holding suffering.

When you become good
at the art of letting sufferings go,
then you'll come to realize how unnecessary it was
for you to drag those burdens around with you.

You'll see that no one else
other than you
was responsible.

The truth is that existence wants your life
to become a festival.

Osho

Refuse to carry the corpse of a mistaken yesterday.

Ernest Holmes

They say that time changes things,
but you actually have to change them yourself.

Andy Warhol

... the injustice...continues to live in the person's mind
just as though it happened five minutes ago...

This means that the painful experience
continues to live in today's reality,
taking up mental and emotional space
that could be given to
more uplifting and productive thoughts.

This is not a healthy state of mind,
for anything that lives makes demands
on the environment in which it lives.

Barbara King

Finish each day and be done with it.
You have done what you could.
Some blunders and absurdities
no doubt crept in;
forget them as soon as you can.

Tomorrow is a new day;
begin it well and serenely,
and with too high a spirit to be cumbered
with your old nonsense.

This day is all that is good and fair.

It is too dear
with its hopes and invitations
to waste a moment on the yesterdays.

Ralph Waldo Emerson

As the Love Activity of God
begins to radiate as an activity of our awareness,
we notice that our tendency
to hold onto grudges and resentment is lessened.

We notice that,
not only do we no longer have the desire
to hold onto resentments,
but now we may even have a desire
to return good for apparent evil…

We may experience the desire
to pray for the individual
and to send good for evil.

This is the real meaning of forgiveness,
to actually give good for negativity.

Michael Beckwith

Forgiveness is the demonstration
that you are the light of the world.

Through your forgiveness
does the truth about your self
return to your memory.

A Course in Miracles

O God,
stitch up my heart with golden thread.

May a new strength grow in the broken places.

Give me courage to feel the pain of betrayal
and the compassion to let it go.

Teach me to forgive myself
as I struggle to forgive others.

And where there are no answers,
may the questions become a prayer.

NGR, a Science of Mind student

8 ONENESS

The diversity and complexity of the universe—interpreted through our senses—confuses us into thinking that we live in a universe of distinct, separate things.

Physics tells us that everything is made of the same stuff—energy as vibration—and that there are no actual boundaries.

All of it is One Thing.

No one is left out. Nothing is an exception. It is impossible to be excluded from this Oneness.

...We are ever eager to mention
this theme of unity to man,
it being the immediate step for him to take.

We would shout in words of fire that oneness *is*.

The Devas of Findhorn Garden

Your union with God
implies your union with everything that lives.
Do not be afraid of this.
Do not shun the thought of it.

...you cannot plunge into the waters of real life
unless you take everyone else in with you.
The universe is one system.

Ernest Holmes

The Tao that can be told is not the eternal Tao.
The name that can be named is not the eternal name.

The nameless is the beginning of heaven and earth.
The named is the mother of ten thousand things.

Ever desireless, one can see the mystery.
Ever desiring, one can see the manifestations.

These two spring from the same source
but differ in name...

Lao Tzu

The game is to be nobody special,
but it does seem that you have to be somebody
before you can be nobody special.

Ram Dass

...the infinite must be a unity.
You cannot have two infinites...
nor can you split the infinite up into fractions...

Now the great fact to be recognized about a unity is that
because it is a single unit,
wherever it is at all the *whole* of it must be...

Spirit is thus omnipresent *in its entirety*,
and it is accordingly logically correct
that at every moment of time
all spirit is concentrated at any point in space
that we may choose to fix our thought upon...

Thomas Troward

The ordinary universe we perceive
is not one universe.

It is the harmony of phases of movements
of an indefinite number of universes...

There is an indefinite number of possibilities.

We exist in all the universe layers simultaneously.

Bob Toben, Jack Sarfatti and Fred Wolf

The journey to God
is merely the reawakening of the knowledge
of *where* you are always,
and *what* you are forever.

It is a journey without distance
to a goal that has never changed.

A Course in Miracles

When I don't know who I am, I serve you.
When I know who I am, I am you.

Ram Dass

Out beyond ideas
of wrongdoing and rightdoing
there is a field.
I'll meet you there.

When the soul lies down in that grass
the world is too full to talk about.

Ideas, language,
even the phrase "each other"
doesn't make any sense.

Jelaluddin Rumi

According to
our current understanding of physics,
every region of space is awash
with different kinds of fields
composed of waves of varying lengths…

When physicists calculate
the minimum amount of energy
a wave can possess,
they find that
every cubic centimeter of empty space
contains more energy
than the total energy of all matter in the known universe!

…Space is not empty. It is full…
and is the ground for the existence of everything,
including ourselves.

Michael Talbot

9 SPIRITUAL MATURITY

As children, we grow into and out of our clothing.

We can grow into and out of different stages of consciousness, too.

Awareness, or spiritual maturity, comes with repeated practice over time.

As much as we may desire *enlightenment*, it doesn't come to us because we are attracted to the idea, or because we've become proficient at talking about it. It comes with living practice.

Spiritual maturity doesn't come with age, yet it's never too late to start our growth in awareness.

It may take a lifetime for us to begin to ripen, or our potential may manifest itself quite quickly, but it never occurs without some kind of personal surrender and persistent attention.

Finally, brothers and sisters, whatever is true,
whatever is noble, whatever is right, whatever is pure,
whatever is lovely, whatever is admirable,
–if anything is excellent or praiseworthy–
think about such things.

St. Paul, Letter to the Philippians 4:8

No one can push a boulder away
while standing on it;
you cannot be free from anxiety
while all the entrances
through which it sneaks in are open.

Atharva Veda, Book XII The Veda of Knowledge

The only person you are destined to become
is the person you decide to be.

Ralph Waldo Emerson

We are powerful beings.
In order to experience our power,
we have to own it and take responsibility for it.
What we give attention to, we nourish.

What we invest time, money, energy, and talent into
is what we are valuing and empowering
for greater growth, strength, and longevity in the future.

We are investing all the time,
but to own our power
and take responsibility for it
we must first consciously admit that we have the power,
and then consciously choose where we focus it
to energize the return we intend to create.

Mary Murray Shelton

The possession of knowledge
does not kill the sense of wonder and mystery.

There is always more mystery.

Anais Nin

We are each of us angels with only one wing and we can fly only by embracing each other.

Luciano de Crescenzo

It is wonderful to know
that your good is at hand.

Your night wanes.
Your dawn is breaking.

There is a living Spirit at the center of your being.
The original Author of all life is in and around you
not a God who *was* but a God who *is*...

Keep the doorway of your mind open.
Feeling, thinking, communing with this Life,
know that It fills you with light and with power.

Ernest Homes

The way we live is the real prayer we are praying.

Our life—with its
actions, beliefs, words, and thoughts
becomes the real prayer of power.

What Creative Law acts upon is the real prayer,
regardless of the words we mouth
in what we think is prayer.

If our life contradicts those words,
the prayer that is made manifest
is the one we have been living,
not the one we have been mouthing.

Mary Murray Shelton

Do the thing and you will have the power.

Ralph Waldo Emerson

10 TRUTH

Sometimes people come to the odd conclusion that *truth* refers to facts that can be weighed and measured with objective, repeatable accuracy.

But often knowing something, discovering a solution, or awakening to an understanding, does not come to us in an orderly, linear way.

A Truth may feel invariably true for me, but not for you. Your Truth may open a sacred path for you that no one else can follow or see.

Truth encompasses not only the known, but also, and more importantly, the unknown.

Truth is so much bigger than the tiny circle we experience as *the known* into which all our facts fit neatly.

...Truth is not the same thing as fact.

Something could be factual, but not true.
And something could be true, but not factual.

Facts are just information, or data points,
about the physical universe.

Truth is much different.

My definition of truth is that
something is true
if it transforms me
and aligns me with God.

And something is ultimate Truth
if it transforms me radically
and aligns me permanently with God.

Sean O'Laoire

Logic will get you from A to B.
Imagination will take you everywhere.

Albert Einstein

All the talents of God are within you.
How could this be otherwise
when your soul derived from his genes?

Hafiz

The Great Way is not difficult
for those who have no preferences.

When love and hate are both absent
everything becomes clear and undisguised.

Make the smallest distinction, however,
and heaven and earth are set infinitely apart.

If you wish to see the truth
then hold no opinions for or against anything.

To set up what you like
against what you dislike
is the disease of the mind.

When the deep meaning of things is not understood,
the mind's essential peace is disturbed to no avail.

Seng T'san, The Third Zen Patriarch

Every great discovery I ever made,
I gambled that the truth was there,
and then I acted on it in faith
until I could prove its existence.

Arthur H. Compton, Nobel Prize physicist

Schubert told a friend that his own creative process
consisted in "remembering a melody"
that no one had ever heard or thought of before.

Maxwell Maltz

Christian, Jew, Muslim, shaman, Zoroastrian,
stone, ground, mountain, river,
each has a secret way
of being with the mystery,
unique and not to be judged.

Jelaluddin Rumi

Most people confuse the Now
with what happens in the Now,
but that's not what it is.

The Now is deeper than what happens in it.

It is the space in which it happens.

Eckhart Tolle

We are energy vibrating as us.

Those vibrations extend outward
from our bodies into the universe.

We *physically* affect our surroundings,
and they, also as energy vibrating,
affect us through the vibrations we exchange.

We are contributing our influence to the universe
and receiving influence from the universe
continuously and constantly.

What kind of influence do we want to be?

Mary Murray Shelton

ABOUT THE AUTHOR

Mary Murray Shelton is an actress, a storyteller, a ceremonialist, and a professional public speaker.

She is passionate about experiencing and expressing ideas through the beauty of words that touch the heart and capture the mind.

She has worked in the clothing, restaurant, and wine industries, done multiple theatre performances and radio interviews, appeared on television, and served in the *Centers for Spiritual Living* ministry since 1986. As a minister, she has served four different congregations in the U.S. and Canada.

Mary has performed ceremonies for hundreds of people: weddings, funerals and memorials, baby blessings, pre-marriage rituals, emptied nest rituals, coming of age rituals and vows renewal ceremonies.

She has given spiritual counsel, been a teacher and mentor, spoken internationally, and is an accomplished retreat facilitator and a published author.

Mary lives in Northern California wine country. She is married and has a married son and a young grandson.

She can be reached through her websites:
http://www.revmary.com
http://www.weddingswithrevmary.weebly.com

INDEX OF THOSE QUOTED

A

A Course in Miracles, 19, 92, 101
Atharva, Book XII–The Veda of Knowledge, 107

B

Meher Baba, 3
Michael Beckwith, 75, 91
Paul Boese, 81
John Seely Brown, 80

C

Julia Cameron, 34
Joseph Campbell, 79
Winston Churchill, 48
Alan Cohen, 30
Arthur H. Compton, 120
e.e. cummings, 11

D

Alfred D'Souza, 4
Ram Dass, 98, 102
Luciano de Crescenzo, 111
Agnes de Mille, 25
The Devas of Findhorn Garden, 95
Tinker Donnelly, 60

E

Thomas A. Edison, 44
Meister Eckhart, 2, 55, 58
Albert Einstein, 117
Ralph Waldo Emerson, 90, 108, 114

F
    Matthew Fox, 16
    Robert Fritz, 27

G
    Benny Golson, 28
    Ellen Goodman, 10
    Martha Graham, 31

H
    Hadith, Sayings of the Prophet, 67
    Hafiz, 52, 118
    Abraham Joshua Heschel, 57
    Ernest Holmes, 20, 41, 68, 72, 77, 87, 96
    Jonathan Lockwood Huie, 82, 84
    Aldous Huxley, 39

J
    Carl Jung, 26

K
    Byron Katie, 85
    Barbara King, 89

L
    Louis L'Amour, 50
    Anne Lamott, 56
    Lao Tzu, 5, 74, 97
    George Leonard, 12
    Stephen Levine, 64
    Raymond Lindquist, 78

M
    Antonio Machado, 76
    Maxwell Maltz, 121
    Joni Mitchell, 22
    Michael Murphy, 12
    Mary Murray Shelton, 18, 24, 35, 45, 109, 113, 124

N
    NGR, 93
    Anais Nin, 110

O
Sean O'Laoire, 116
Osho, 86

P
Karl Paulnack, 33
Hugh Prather, 70

R
Harriet Rubin, 49
Jelaluddin Rumi, 6, 7, 15, 21, 29, 32, 38, 46, 54, 63, 65, 69, 83, 103, 122

S
Jack Sarfatti, 100
Seng T'san, 119
Huston Smith, 8
St. Paul, 9, 106
Brian Swimme, 14, 66

T
Michael Talbot, 104
The Talmud, 17
Bernie Taupin, 71
Bob Toben, 100
Eckhart Tolle, 36, 59, 123
Thomas Troward, 99

U
Unity Prayer for Protection, 53
Unknown, 43

V
George M. Van Valkenburg, Jr., 42

W
Andy Warhol, 88
Alan Watts, 61
Fred Wolf, 100

Z
Zen Buddhism, 47

Made in the USA
San Bernardino, CA
08 October 2014